EPHESUS

DOĞAN GÜMÜŞ

Translation
Christine M. Thomas

DOĞU
YAYINLARI

TABLE OF CONTENTS

The most spectacular building of Ephesus has to be the Grand Theatre.

THEATRE

GENERAL INTRODUCTION

The Ephesians believed that it was the beautiful Amazonian queen Ephesia who had founded their city. Strabo and Pausanias held the same opinion. The Amazons were extremely ferocious warrior women. Yet the origin of their name is unkown. It is said that they originally came from north-east Anatolia and that their capital was in the region of the present-day towns of Fatsa and Ordu. According to mythology, tne Amazons are supposed to have been the children of the god of war, Ares (which would explain their bellicose character) and of the spirit of tne rivers, Harmonia, or of the goddess Aphrodite. They were excellent horsewomen and used bows and arrows, hatchets, lances and shields. It has even been claimed that they constituted the first cavalry. In particular, they are supposed to have been the forerunners of feminism. They hated men, despising them and using them as slaves. They would burn one of their own breasts in order better to use the bow and arrow and would mate with the men from neighbouring cities and then kill them. They once carried out a general massacre simply because they had heard that the male god Zeus was rising in power, and that, moreover, men had started claiming that it was they who played the most important role in mating. They therefore decided to masscare them all, in order to avoid a male uprising, and amputated their sex organs, which they presented as an offering to the mother-goddess; In order to make sure that the male children would not later revolt, they broke their arms. (We do not know if this story is just the product of male imagination; but at Ephesus, even the men held the Amazons in the greatest esteem.)

In another myth, on the other hand, the founding of Ephesus is attributed to Androklos, the son of Kodros, the king of Athens. An interesting story about this is told through the friezes of the temple of Hadrian, in the Street of the Kourefes at Ephesus. After his father's death, Androklos was obliged by troubles in his country to go abroad. As in every legend, he turned to the Oracles of the sacred temple at Delphi, in order to ask them where he could build a new city. The Oracles, as usual, gave an unintelligible answer: "This place will be pointed out to you by a fish; a boar will show you the way." (It is aid that Androclus, helpless in Anatolia, sent a messenger to Delphi, and thus received this answer). One day, while they were roasting some fish they had caught, one of the fish jumped into a bush: a boar which happened to be there was frightened and started to run away. Androklos remembered the words of the Oracle and followed the boar. After a long chase, Androklos struck it with his arrow. From that moment the location of his future city was determined.

Androclus and his dog.

4

According to Herodotos, the original inhabitants of Ephesus were the Karians and the Lelegians. The Karians' capital was at Halikarnassos (near present-day Bodrum), they considered themselves the indigenous population of Anatolia and were proud of being the most ancient tenants of these lands. As for the Lelegians, they had emigrated to Anatolia from Thrace and the Aegean isles. (Some researchers push their hypotheses further, to claim that Ephesus and the town of Apasas quoted in Hittite writing were one and the same.) Thus the legends told of the beginnings of Ephesus are mutually contradictory. But all of them have been over-shadowed by important discoveries made during modern archeological excavations which were started in Ephesus in 1869 and have continued with success for the last 122 years. The most ancient settlement brought to light by these excavations was found in the Commercial Agora, which we also call the lower Agora.

Here, remains of architecture dating from the 8th-7th Century BC were found 8 metres below the surface of the earth, and it was concluded that this was the locataion of the archaic Ephesus.

A Mycenaean necropolis was also discovered, by chance, during the construction of a car-park near the Church of St John, in 1954. The Mycenaean ceramic vessels displayed in the "funerary relics" room of the museum were retrieved from this necropolis. These remains, dating from the 14th and 15th century BC, are the most ancient to have been found at Ephesus. However, the location of the Mycenaean settlement has not been found.

Only 4-5% of the city has been successfully excavated. Doubtless far more ancient settlement locations will be uncovered in years to come.

It is likely that Androklos arrived in Anatolia after the Trojan wars and that the story of the fish and the boar is pure fiction. He occupied Ephesus and its environs and expelled much of its Karian and Lelegian population. Those who

The Trajan fountain.

stayed, he made his subjects: Androklos, being a good warrior, expanded his domain in a short space of time. Morever, the population of his kingdom, which lived off agriculture and stock breeding, became rich through commerce.

Regardless of all this progress, the natives of Anatolia, the Karians, their pride having been affronted by these campaigns of colonisation, fought back against the new arrivals. At one time, they quarrelled with Priene, a neighbour and ally of Ephesus. Priene requested Androklos' assistance. He had had enough of the Karians anyway and wanted to teach them a good lesson. He attacked the Karians. At a time when everyone was expecting Androclus' definitive victory, the news of his death sent the whole town into mourning.

Of the history of Ephesus, a period of about 400 years, including Androklos' rule and the years following his death, remains in shadow. We know nothing of the life of the people nor of the architectural styles of the towns of this peirod. Everything concerning this era is buried under the earth. Before Androklos, the city had been ruled by kings, and after him came a great dynasty called the Tyrants. With the passage of time, they grew away from the people and around 600 BC, had to bow to pressure from the populace and accept the creation of a parliament. The name of Kouretes, that is, holy, was given to the members of this assembly. Every year, six members of the Kouretes were replaced.

The 7th century BC brought a change in the destiny of Ephesus and of all of Ionia. The cities which, apart from the occasional squabble, lived in peace and harmony, suddeny became the focus of foreign forces which, fighting against each other, caused damage to the Ionians. First it was the Kimmerians who attacked. It is unknown whether the Kimmerians succeeded in entering the town of Ephesus after this attack, which took place during the seventh century BC. From the remains of Ephesus, we know that they annihilated the temple of

The Temple of Hadrian

Artemis (Artemision). (The Kimmerians left a few works of art, such as the ivory figure of a ram. These are exhibited at the museum of Ephesus).

The 6th century BC, with its celebrated poets such as Kallinos, Hipponax and the erudite Herakleitos, was one of the most brilliant eras of Ephesus. Whether for her culture, for her social life, or for her port, the renown of Ephesus rapidly spread throughout Anatolia, the Aegean isles, and to Athens. In the meantime Kroisos, the all-powerful king of the Lydians who had made Sardis their capital, first conquered Ephesus, before embarking on the conquest of the whole of Anatolia.

The Ephesians were not in the least expecting this attack. In any case, they did not have enough force to repel the Lydians, and the only place they had as a refuge was the Artemision. They used strong ropes to attach the temple to the walls of the town. Thus the whole of the town would come under the protective influence of the temple. Even the most fearful bandits became untouchable once they had entered the temple's sphere of protection. Yet the power of Artemis proved not to be strong enough to halt Kroisos, who entered the city.

Contrary to their fear, the Lydians treated the Ephesians well. They were only obliged to pay a negligible sum in taxes and continued to live without the slightest repression. Further, Kroisos for the first time instigated work for the prosperity of Ephesus. He forced the population to leave Koressos, where they were settled, and to go and live in a newly-built location nearby and in spite of some resistance, he met with success. Meanwhile construction work on the temple of Artemis continued. He contributed to this and presented the temple with some pedestals of exceptional beauty. One of these boasted his own signature. (These pedestals were taken to the British Museum in the course of the excavations started in 1869).

Thus even Artemis failed to stop Kroisos; but soon a danger which he could not overcome awaited him: the Persians, who

Busts of Lysimachus and Greath Alexander.

had set out from their country with a great army, were appoaching the Lydian borders.

The first aim of the Persains was to provoke a bit of trouble within Lydia. They sent ambassadors to Sardis and the Ionian cities and suggested that they should rebel against the Lydians. The Ionians were so trusting of Kroisos that they rejected this proposition. But the Persian king Cyrus conquered kroisos and advanced towards Ionia. In a panic, the twelve city-states gathered together and agreed to join forces and send ambassadors to Cyrus. The latter received them and, having listened to them, told the following anecdote: "A piper saw some fish in the sea. He thought he would be able to draw them out from the water by playing his pipe to them. He showed off his skill, but in vain. He then cast his fishing net into the sea and caught all the fish, which started wriggling on the ground. So the piper said to them: I played you my best melodies, but you would not listen. So there's no point in wriggling now." The answer was clear enough. The Persians rejected the offer of peace extended by the Ionians. All the Ionian cities apart from Miletos therefore decided to join forces in opposing the Persians. They also sought help from Sparta. But in 547 BC, Harpagos, one of Cyrus' commanders, conquered the whole of western Anatolia.

The Persians allowed the people of countries they had conquered to practise their own religion and didn't interfere in their internal affairs. Nevertheless, they applied a new system to Anatolia. They founded the Ionian Satrapy by joining together cities such as Karia, Lykia, Pamphylia and Ionia. Although daily life in Ephesus and the other Ionian cities was enriched, hostilities against the Persains increased with time. In particular, following the rise in taxes at the time of Cambyses and Darius, successors to Cyrus, the Ionians united and, in the year 500 BC, rebelled in a movement to which history has given the name "the Ionian insurrection"; in a short space of time, they conquered Sardis, the centre of the Persian Satrapy. They even destroyed the temple of Kybele. The Persians, who had offered no resistance, were shocked, for they had never carried out any massacres, nor destroyed temples. This rebellion lasted 6 years and concluded with the victory of the Persians in the region of the isle of Lade, offshore from Miletos. (In the course of fighting, a tragedy occurred, in which the Ephesians massacred their own allies: a group of Chians, fleeing the

Persian army, arrived at Ephesus in the night of the Thesmophoria Festival, a celebration attended by the women of the city. The Ephesians, seeing them fully armed, naturally thought they had come to kidnap and the womenfolk, slaughtered them to the last man.)

The Persians reconquered Ionia and, in reprisal for what had been done at Sardis, pillaged and sacked the Ionian cities. The Ionians and the Western Anatolians, yet again finding themselves having to surrender unconditionally, wanted at all cost to rid themselves of the Persians. But alone, they could not. Help could come only from Athens or Sparta, unsubdued by the Persians and in continual conflict with them. Together, they conquered the Persians in 479 BC and expelled them from Anatolia. In 478 BC, they founded the "Maritime Union of Attica-Delos." According to this union, the states would provide money or ships to Athens in case of war. In the cities, an Athenian garrison was set up. A large sum of money, made up of donations to Apollo, was handed over to the service of the goddess Athena.

In actual fact, the Ephesians, who didn't much like war, contributed only by providing money; in spite of this they were not at all pleased with the situation. They were still paying taxes and were still not free in the running of their foreign affairs. In the meantime, war broke out between Sparta and Athens, in 431 BC. During the course of this war, which was to be called the Peloponesian war, Ephesus first sided with Athens, and later with Sparta against Athens; an intriguing fact considering the enmity which had existed between the Ephesians and the Spartans for years. The Spartans won the war and handed over Anatolia to the Persians, in accordance with an agreement already concluded between these two countries. Ephesus and the other Ionian cities, without quite grasping what was happening to them, submitted to the second Persian era, which dirctely preceded the arrival of Alexander the Great in Anatolia.

In spite of so many wars and invasions, there were no vast changes in the social life of the Ioians and Ephesians. In fact, in Ionia, women and men enjoyed much greater rights than those of the countries which conquered them. For example, in many countries, but not in Anatolia, foreigners had practically no rights. They could buy neither land nor houses. It was difficult for them to marry a woman from that country and even if they were able to get married, their children were not considered citizens of that country. They were not allowed the vote, either. A foreigner setting in Ionia, on the other hnd, was considered a citizen of the town. Women received education. Among their numbers can be counted poets, scholars and admirals. At Priene and in the Anatolian cities, there were even female judges. Following the reconquering of Anatolia by Alexander, women are seen joining in political intrigue.

Having become king of Macedonia at a very young age on the death of his father, Alexander first re-established the unity of the Greek peninsula and then made his way towards Anatolia to chase away the Persians who had always been a thorn in the Ionians' side. He crossed the Dardanelles and put the Persians to rout. After a four-day voyage, he arrived in Ephesus, where he was greeted with much ceremony. (In fact the Ephesians were at a loss as to what to do what with all these invasions and re-conquests).

The Ephesians were paying taxes to the Persians. Alexander ordered them to pay these taxes to the temple of Artemis, and expressed the desire to oversee its construction.The Ephesians opposed this so Alexander went on his way and fought the Persians and most of the Anatolian cities, which resisted him. When he died at a very young age, his Empire fell into disarray which lasted a very long time before his dominion was divided up among his generals. Lysimachus had as his

Left: statue
Righ,
the Celsus
Library

share the area including Ephesus (290 BC). (It was Lysimachos who took with him a stash of gold worth five million talents and hid it at Pergamon giving orders to his officer Philetaeros to guard it). His greatest achievement in Ephesus was to move the town. For the town, he chose the valley between Mount Koressos and Mount Pion and had building start immediately. In fact, he had a point. Many Ephesians were dying of epidemics of malaria. The losses were more severe than those caused by the wars. The alluvia brought by the river Cayster (Küçük Menderes) with time formed a swamp in the port and the mosquitoes caused the spread of the disesae. The Ephesians had not been able to find a remedy, yet they still refused to leave their ancient city, claiming that the new city was too far from the temple of Artemis (in fact, the distance was 2 km). Moreover Lysimachos had namled the new town after his wife Arsinoe. The town would no longer be called Ephesus. So the Ephesians refused to budge. However, Lysimachos, having

spent a considerable amount on the building of the new town, did not intend to be disobeyed. Finally, by a stroke of genius, he solved the problem. When the rainy season started, the Ephesians' houses were all flooded and became uninhabitable. Their owners had no choice but to move to the new town. (It was only much later that they learned the cause of flooding: the town's sewers had quite simply been blocked by order of the king).

As mentioned above, the women of Ephesus had by this time started their political intrigues. It was now impossible to control the young and beautiful Arsinoe, Lysimachos' wife. Her caprices were endless. She had succeeded in having her name given to Ephesus and now she wanted to be all-powerful. There was only one obstacle in her way: Agathokles, the son of Lysimachus' first wife, and whom the people adored. She stirred up Lysimachos against his son and had him killed. The Ephesians, who did

The
Theatre room

not like Arsinoe, never forgave her this action. Agathokles' mother and certain commanders sought refuge with the Syrian king Seleucus II, who, profitting from the situation, declared war on Lysimachos. Troughout the war, the Ephesians did all they could to help Seleukos. Lysimachos was defeated and died on the battleground. As for Arsione, we do not know what happened to her. From now on, Ephesus was under the domition of the Syrian king who ruled over the whole of Antochia. Ephesus suffered for a long time as a result of the skirmishes between this kingdom and the Egpytians, and several times changed hands. But from time to time were periods of peace and understanding between the Seleucids and Egyptians.

One such period was particularly interesting for Ephesus: the Egyptians knew that it was the queen Laodice who had stirred up her husband Antiochos II, King of the Seleucids, against them. Ptolemy let Antiochos know that he was prepared to make peace and to offer him his beautiful daughter Berenice with her dowry, as long as he divorced his wife. Antiochos did so and exiled Laodike to Ephesus. Since she was a very ambitious woman, she tried out all her tricks to become queen again. Before ten years had passed, Antiochos came to Ephesus to see his ex-wife and his children. Laodike poisoned him and made her son king. Later, the Egyptians seized Ephesus and such squabbles continued until the Roman period.

The Romans obtained Ephesus without fighting, as a legacy from the king of Pergamon, in 133 BC. During the early years they exploited the Ephesians to such an extent that these would gladly have accepted the Persians' yoke. Inflation and daily increases in taxes strained the Ephesians' patience. But Rome was very powerful. So all the Ionians could do was wait for a saviour. He appeared in the year 88 BC, Mithridates, the young and powerful king of the empire of Pontos, on

Peristyle of house A.

13

the Black Sea Coast. Filled with hatred for the Romans and backed by the Anatolians, he conquered his enemies in a short time. He was so blinded by his lust for vengeance that of the 100,000 Romans in Anatolia (most of whom were in Ephesus), he had 80,000 massacred. The Ephesians were unhappy about this, for they ran the risk of being faced later with the same fate as the Romans. Indeed, a while later, the general Zenobios ordered the Ephesians to gather together in the theatre. The Ephesians immediately sent an ambassador to the genral, asking him to leave his soldiers outside the city and to come alone. Not suspecting a trap, Zenobios entered the city and was immediately killed. Rebelling for the first time in history, the Ephesians launched a surprise attack on the Pontic headquarters and massacred all the soldiers. This took place in the year 87 BC. Three years after this revolt, the Roman army, under the command of Sulla, conquered Mithritades and was again master of Anatolia.

Ephesus, having been under Roman occupation for centuries, gained significance after the year 27 BC. This was the date on which Octavius, by decree of the Senate, took the title Augustus and made Ephesus the capital of the Asian province in place of Pergamon. Thus Ephesus became one of the five great cities of he of Roman Empire, the permanent residence of the Governor of Rome, a centre of commerce and the most important metropolis of the Asian province.

The city's most brilliant years were between the first and the second centuries BC, when she became the second greatest city of the East, after Alexandria. The Ephesians' daily life changed as they grew even richer. Apart from their native language, they also learned Latin. The orders of the Emperor and the new laws were written and displayed in two languages. In their religion, however,

little had changed, expect the names of a few gods. Certain foreign gods had been accepted (such as the Egyptian gods) and, most important of all, the Roman emperors had been deified and temples erected in their honour. In the city, there were also monotheistic Jews, and while they were trying to spread their religion, Jesus was in Jerusalem gathering support for a new religion, Christianity. After the crucfixion the apostles left Jerusalem to preach Christianity. This was a time of historical significance for Ephesus. First, St John arrived in Ephesus, accompanied by the Holy Virgin. He gathered around him a great number of followers in the Aegean region. (Both Mary and John died and were buried at Ephesus). It was St Paul who played the major role in the propogation of Christianity. When he reached Ephesus in 53, he found a small group of Christians there. He baptized them in the name of Christ and organized them. Through his efforts the number of Christians increased considerably.

Church of Saint Jonh.

This disturbud certain tradesmen more than it did the idolators. Among these tradesmen was one named Demetrios, who made and sold silver statues of Artemis; having come close to losing his livelihood, he publicly declared that no-one could be as great as Artemis of Ephesus. In a short space of time he convinced thousands of people. They gathered and walked towards the theatre, shouting. Their numbers swelled and the streets of Ephesus rang with the name of Artemis. In fact, many of them were not even sure why they were shouting, and chaos reigned over the city. Next, they assembled in the theatre and started beating any Christians they could lay their hands on. The city was gripped by insurrection. Finally the authorities re-established the peace. (All this fighting was like the death cry of Artemis, the thousand-year-old goddess of Anatolia: over the next few centuries, her statues, her temples, everything which belonged to her was tobe annihilated). Paul left for Macedonia.

This was the Golden Age of Ephesian architecture. All the buildings of Ephesus, entirely destroyed by an earthquake in the year 17 BC, were restored and, with new temples, fountains, and other buildings, the city had become even more resplendent.

The only disorder which reigned in the city was due to the increasing number of Christians. After suffering many vicissitudes, they finaly gained acceptance and Christianity became the religion of the Empire in the fourth century. However, they were divided by a disagreement. Nestorius of Antioch claimed that the Virgin Mary was not the mother of God, but of Christ (that is, of a human being); and he was gathering a tremendous amount of followers. Having become Patriarch of Constatinople (Istanbul), Nestorius tried to have his thesis accepted throughout the Church. But his adversaries kept contradicting him. Confusion mounted to such an extent that the Emperor decided to call a

The Church of Saint John and the Castle.

Council. The gathering of the Council took place in the church of St Mary at Ephesus in 431. At this gathering, in which over 200 bishops participated, the thesis of Cyril, Bishop of Alexandria, emerged victorious (Mother Mary is the mother of God) and Nestorius was exiled to Egypt. In spite of this, the arguing did not cease. 18 years later, another Council was held, which has been handed down to history under tne name of Latrocinium Ephesinium (the Robbers' Council) for the Alexanderians had their thesis accepted by force. Nonetheless, these two Councils made a very important contribution to the city of Ephesus: it was noted in the minutes of these meetings that this was the resting place of St John and St Mary.

Another significant event of the same century was the second move of the city. The Ephesians left their port, which had become swampy, and went to settle in the vicinity of the Church of St John. After the division of the Roman Empire, Ephesus, being within the Eastern Roman Empire, gradually lost importance.

The city was weakened by attacks by urban pirates and by the Arabs; many Ephesians were obliged to leave the city.

After the elevenht century, she had become nothing more that a little village, referred to as "Hagio Theologos", which was occupied by the Aydınoğulları (a Turkish tribe). Under their rule, she saw another period of prosperity. She was adorned with Turkish edifices such as mosques both small and great, hamams, and caravansarays. During the time of the Ottoman Empire, she was completely abandoned.

In our day and age, of all the antique cities of the world, Ephesus is the best preserved. She is situated between Kuşadası and selçuk, at equal distance between the two towns.

Statue of Artemis.

TEMPLE OF ARTEMIS

The most significant factor which brought such fame to the city of Ephesos was without doubt the mother-goddess Artemis and her temple. Artemis was a goddess of Anatolian origin and, until the time when she appeared on the stage of history, she was called Kybele, Kybele or Hepa. In fact, statuettes of goddesses have been found in Anatolia belonging to far earlier times, the most ancient having been found at Çatalhöyük and dated 7000 years BC. All of them, whether it be the statuettes of Çatalhöyük or those of Hacılar dated 6000 BC, bear striking resemblance and symbolize fertility, with their wide hips and large breasts. Their names, however, remain unknown.

Another mystery is how the worship of Artemis was born in Ephesus. At the beginning of the second millennium BC, it seems that a sacred stone existed at Ephesus. This was probably a meteorite. Then the Amazons made their appearance in history. According to the story, the Amazons, using the wood of a palm-tree, fashioned the first statuette of the mother-goddess. Again at an unspecified date, this mother-goddess is supposed to have taken on human form.

Artemis was considered the most powerful of all the goddesses, for she possessed the characteristics and, above all, the powers of many of the other goddesses. She spread abundance and fertility, she came to the aid of women in childbirth, protected nature; she was the goddess of hunting and of the moon. She ruled over fate and over the Zodiac signs of humans, brought rain and made the earth fertile. With all these attributes, the fame of Artemis grew from day to day and spread even as far as Marseille, through the sailors who often frequented the port of Ephesus.

At Ephesus, the worship of Artemis was always considered superior to that of other gods and this is why, apart from the Temple of Artemis, only a few other temples were erected, devoted to Egyptian gods who promised resurrection. During the Roman era, temples were also built in the name of the deified emperors.

For the Ephesians the power of Artemis and of her people was inexhaustible. On this point, the story was handed down from generation to generation that it was Artemis who one night had personally put the architrave, weighing several tons, in place over the columns which were over 20 metres in height. Nevertheless, several events roused

Statue of the Blessed Virgin.

suspicion among the Ephesians concerning the strength of Artemis: during the Lydian attack, they had drawn a rope between the temple and the city, in the belief that this would prevent Kroisos from getting through, but in vain. In the year 356 BC, on the night of the birth of Alexander, the temple was destroyed by a lunatic called Herostratus. Later it was said that on that night, Artemis had gone to assist at the birth of Alexander.

At its apogee, the temple was run without outside intervention and preserved its autonomy. The man in charge of its administration was the High Priest Megabysos, castrated according to the cult of Cybele. He had been chosen from among the natives of Asia Minor and had virgins at his service. The Kouretes were another order of priests who served Artemis. They were semi-gods, supposed to have intimate relaitons with Zeus. During the childbirth of Leto, Artemis' mother, at which they were supposed to have assisted, they apparently prevented Hera from hearing the cries of the new-born babe by the noise they made. Each year, the Kouretes went with ceremony to Ortygia, the birthplace of Artemis (7 km to the south of Ephesus, on what is now the road to Kuşadası), to celebrate her birthday. In these kinds of ceremonies and festivities, nother order of priests figures: the acrobatae. They would lead the procession with fantastic displays. In fact , at the temple, the collaboration between the priests and the priestesses was rather interesting: there were priestesses whose duty was to prepare the clothes of the goddess (the Kosmiterae), there were also those who would display the clothes and jewellery of Artemis during the sacred ceremonies (Kosmoforoi) and those responsible for the precious objects belonging to the goddess (the Khristoforoi). Apart from these, the "Zigostates" measured and weighed all objects taken from or brought to the temple. The "Himnodoi" took the place of latter-day choirs. The "Hierokiris" gave sermons, while the "Spondopoios" were the priests or priestesses of the goddess, who sprayed holy water on the ground. There were also "Grammateis" who would write the answers given by the goddess to questions asked by her followers.

One of the most interesting characteristics of the temple was that it held the function of a bank. The Megabysos was in charge of the budget of the temple; he gave credit and received the gifts made to the goddess.

This temple was one of the seven wonders of the world, alongside the Mausoleum of Halikarnassos, the statue of Zeus at Olympia, the Pharos at Alexandria, the Hanging Gardens of Babylon, the Colossus of Rhodes and the Pyramids of Egypt. Of the Artemision, all that remains is one column, which can be seen to the left of the road leading from Selçuk to Kuşadası. The column was reconstituted by superimposing pieces found in the vicinity. The single cause of the destruction of this sumptuous edifice was the rivalry which existed between the various religions and beliefs. The first Christians of Ephesus, having suffered violent persecution, bore a severe grudge against the protectress of Ephesus and her temple. Once they had gained the upper hand, they annihilated the temple. Part of its architectural material was re-used in the building of Hagia Sophia in Istanbul. Other pieces were carved up at quarries. Shortly thereafter, the alluvia brought by the Cayster river covered up the rest of the temple and wiped out all traces of it. Research made by the English engineer Wood in 1863 bore no results: but in 1869, he discovered an inscription in a

Temple of Artemis, Church of Saint John and castle.

TEMPLE OF ARTEMIS

theatre. On deciphering it, he understood that the sacred items used during performances at the theatre had been brought into the city via the Magnesian Gate along the Sacred Way, after having been taken from the temple. First he found the Magnesian Gate, then he located the famous temple by following the sacred way which led to it. Over the following years, excavations were intensified and several small pieces found were carried off to England. In 1895, the Austrian Insitute of Archeology took over the excavations under the directions of D.G. Hogarth, until 1905. Nowadays, work on the Artemision is in the hands of Dr. Bammer.

According to Strabo, the Artemision, a precious example of Ionian architecture, was destroyed and rebuilt seven times. The latest excavations confirm this statement. Whereas of old it was situated on the edge of the sea, the temple is now five km inland. The first temple, to which we refer to as the archaic temple, was destroyed in the seventh century BC by the Kimmerians. During excavation, geometrically shaped vessels were found, along with ornamental objects made of gold and ivory dating from this era. In the year 570 BC, the inhabitants of Ephesus decided to erect a temple more majestic than that of Hera at Samos. They gave the job of building it to the architect Chersiphron of Knossos, his son Metagenes and the architect Theodoros, who had proved his talent in the construction of the temple of Hera at Samos on land which, like that of Ephesus, was swamp-ridden. The foundations of the temple were placed over a layer of coal which was covered in leather. In the end, a beautiful construction of 55.1 m x 115.14 m appeared. It was the largest temple built of marble. A double row of 19 m high columns surrounded the walls. The

"columnae caeletae", that is, the 36 front columns were, decorated with friezes donated by Kroisos.
It is said that a certain Herostratos, in order to immortalize his name, burned the temple in 356 BC, the night of the birth of Alexander. However, the famous writer C.S. Karaağaç (called the fisherman of Halikarnassos) interprets this event in a different manner. "...It has been claimed that a madman, named Herostratos, burned the temple in order that his name should figure in an important historical event. In fact, it would be impossible for a single man to do this. There were guards inside and outside the temple. Only the door, the stairs and ceiling were made of wood. In order to set the temple on fire, Herostratos would have had to arrive with a torch and a ladder without being noticed. That would have been impossible. Then the smoke would certainly have been seen by the guards or the people living in the vicinity. What

Column of the Artemision.

seems more logical is that the priests, having stolen the jewels of the temple, might have set fire to it and accused a madman unable to defend himself."

The Ephesians restored the temple according to the original architect's plan.Not thirty years had passed before Alexander entered Ephesus, having conquered the Persians. He had of course heard of the fame of Artemis of Ephesus.

The temple was not yet completed. Alexander promised the Ephesians that he would cover all the remaining construction costs as long as his name was carved on the façade. In spite of being short of money and not in a good position to refuse Alexander's offer, they found a subterfuge: they claimed that it would not be right for one god to have a temple built to the glory of another. Thus they had honoured Alexander by attributing to him the title of god.They

finished the work on the temple by themselves. It was 155 metres in lengthand 55 metres wide.

The Ephesians summoned all the famous engineers, architects and painters of their day, so that their temple should be unique.Among them Polykleitos, Phidias, Cresilas, Cydon and Pharadmon eachsculpted a statue of an Amazon each for the temple.

The Ephesians couldn't choose the best statue, so they left the choice to the artists. They held a vote and Polykleitos gained the majority (a copy of it made during the Roman era still exists). Scopas worked on the relief of one of the columns and another sculptor, Praxiteles, executed the altar.

This magnificent temple was destroyed by the Goths in 265 CE. Although it was subsequently restored, it was annihilated by the Christians for the

Reconstrucction
of
the Artemision.

Bust of Eros.
Right:
the Prytaneum.

THE BUST OF EROS

22

ANCIENT SITES

During Roman times, the ancient city founded by Lysimachos, situated between Panayirdaqi, Bülbüldaqi, and the Temple of Artemis, became a metropolis with 200,000 inhabitants, which measured 316 hectares.

Since hostile attacks were always a possibility, the **city walls** were built in the third century BCE (Before the Common Era), after Lysimachos refounded the city. The walls are 9 km long and 10 meters high, and were constructed with watch towers. They are only in a relatively good state of preservation along the slopes of the mountains. One entered the city through two main gates. The **Koressos Gate** is located between the Vedius Gymnasium and the stadium. The second gate is the **Magnesian Gate**, on the way to the House of Mary. This gate was constructed at the same time as the city walls, and was converted into a monumental triumphal arch with three arches in the first century CE (of the Common Era). The gate also forms part of the sacred way leading to the temple of Artemis. The Koressos Gate allowed access to the harbor, and was the beginning of the royal highway leading to the interior of Anatolia.

In the city plan, which is laid out on a grid pattern (the Hippodamian plan), there are three main streets. These are the harbor street, or Arkadiane, which runs from the harbor to the theater, the marble road, which lies between the theater and the Library of Celsus, and Kouretes Street, which runs between the library and Domitian Street.

In the Roman period, the agoràs, that is, the city squares, played a great role as meeting places and centers of trade. One of these was the **state agora**, which was constructed on top of its Hellenistic predecessor in the first century BCE; it measures 160 by 56 meters. This agora was renovated in the first century by the addition of government buildings. Stoas bounded the state agora on three sides; in

Photoes on the next page: Baths of Varius, Basilica, Odeion. and a general overview

its center stood a rectangular **temple** dedicated either to **Augustus or Isis**. This temple had ten columns on its long sides, and six on its short sides. Its façade contained a statue group that portrayed the legend of Odysseus and Polyphemos. This statue group was later incorporated into the Fountain of Pollio, and now stands on display in the Ephesus Museum.

In the northern area of the agora, a three-aisled **basilica**, built in the first century BCE, fulfilled the function of an exchange. This basilica had a tripartite, monumental gate that opened onto a stoa leading to the Baths of Varius.

Immediately behind this basilica stood such important buildings as the prytaneion and odeon (bouleuterion). The **prytaneion** was a sort of city hall, serving religious purposes, official receptions, and banquets. The eternal fire, which symbolized the hearths of Ephesus, burned within it. Members of prominent families of the city cared for it so that its fire never died out. The greater part of this complex dates to the Augustan age,

although its construction was only completed in the third century CE. A courtyard surrounded by stoas stood in front of it. Towards the back, there was a large, roofed space, in the center of which the base of an altar is still recognizable. In the two additional rooms that lie west of this main hall, archaeologists discovered two beautiful statues of Artemis; these are now on display in the Ephesus Museum.

The **bouleuterion** is a small theater with a cavea, orchestra, and skene. A diazoma divides the semicircular cavea horizontally. The structure probably had a roof, and could seat 1400 people. The city government held its sessions in the bouleuterion, but it also served as an **odeon** for concerts. The building was a gift from Publius Vedius Antoninus in the middle of the second century CE. Between the bouleuterion and the prytaneion stand the **temples of the divinized Julius and the goddess Roma**. Augustus probably granted the permission to build these temples during his official visit in 29 BCE. These ruler cult temples represented a special honor in those times. Roma is the goddess that symbolized the city of Rome. The Divus (divinized) Julius is Julius Caesar, who was elevated to semi-divine status after his death, and was the adoptive father of the emperor Augustus.

The ruins to the right of the odeon belong to the **Baths of Varius**, dating to the high Roman empire. Baths played an important role in Roman social life. This was not only the place to refresh oneself from everyday life, but also to find entertainment and to conduct engaging political and philosophical discussions. In some of the richer Roman cities, the poor could enjoy the baths free of cost. According to Selahattin Erdemgil, the inhabitants of Ephesus came to the baths with their retinue in the afternoon, and stayed there for hours. Certain customs were in effect in the baths. Visitors would disrobe in the apodyterium (dressing room) and then went to the sudotorium to enjoy the sauna. They refreshed

Memmius Monument and relief of Nike
Right Domitian Street and surrounding area

themselves in the frigidarium (cold room) before entering the hottest room, the caldarium. Bathers met for conversation in the tepidarium (warm room) and then went for a swim in the natatorium. The Baths of Varius were frequently renovated. With the all the rooms named above, it provides a beautiful example of Roman architecture.

From the prytaneion, a path leads to **Domitian Street**. On the either side of this path are two column drums. The one on the left depicts the naked Hermes, and the one on the right, Hermes holding a goat by the horns.

North of Domitian Street is a monumental commemorative structure with four façades, the **Memmius Monument**. Memmius, the grandson of the dictator Sulla, constructed it in the first century CE. The blocks that contain the figures of his father, Gaius, and grandfather, Sulla, are still well preserved. A square fountain lies northwest of this memorial. Statues of the emperors of that time, the tetrarchs Diocletian, Maximian, Constantius I, and Galerius (293-305 CE) once stood around this fountain. In the middle of Domitian Street is a round **monument** that once stood elsewhere, and was later brought here from some other location. The **relief of Nike** to the side, likewise, once formed part of the Gate of Herakles.

A two-story structure on the side nearest the agora has a high, broad arch that faces the shops along Domitian Street. This is the most beautiful fountain in the city, the **Fountain of Pollio**, which Pollio donated; it was renovated in 93 CE. The statue group of Polyphemos that once stood over the basin comes from the Temple of Isis (Augustus), and is now on display in the Ephesus Museum.

For cities in the Roman empire, it was a great honor to receive permission to build an imperial cult temple. This aroused great competition and resulted in not a few intrigues. The emperor could also subsequently withdraw this right, called a "neokorate" ("temple wardenship"). Ephesus was granted this right many

times; during the imperial period, the first neokorate came from the emperor Domitian. The Ephesians wished to reciprocate appropriately, and so erected a 6 to 7 meter statue of him in front of the cella (main room) of the **Temple of Domitian**. This temple once stood on a terrace south of Domitian Street. It was a prostyle temple with eight columns on the short sides and thirteen on the long sides. Four additional columns stood in front of the cella. The altar was U-shaped; a flight of stairs led up to it. Domitian was a rather unpopular emperor; his own servants finally murdered him. This caused great confusion in Ephesus, since Domitian was, after all, the first Roman emperor to grant them the signal honor of building an imperial neokorate temple; they owed him a debt of gratitude. Because of his unpopularity, Ephesus stood to lose the right to build such temples.They turned the difficulty to good account by re-dedicating the temple to his father, Vespasian, and honoring him from that point onward.

The ruins of the **Fountain of Gaius Laecanius Bassus**, a structure from the first century CE (of the Common Era), can be seen near Domitian Street. The fountain consists of a colonnaded courtyard and two basins. The statues that decorated the fountain are now on display in the Ephesus Museum.

Kouretes Street, one of the main streets of ancient Ephesus, begins west of Domitian Street. The **Gate of Herakles** once opened onto this street. The upper story of this two-story structure contained six columns; two of these still stand in the area of the gate. Colonnaded galleries, the floors of which were decorated by mosaics, lined both sides of Kouretes Street; behind these were various shops. Statues once stood in front of the galleries. As is common in Ephesus, the pavement in front of the buildings is inconsistent and uneven. Reconstruction work after the various earthquakes was often carried out with whatever materials could be salvaged, and resulted in this motley appearance.

The first structure on the right side that one encounters when walking in the direction of the Library of Celsus is the **Fountain of Trajan**, built around 104 CE. It consisted of a two-story façade, decorated with columns and statues, and a basin. The statue of Trajan once stood in the central niche. Although the fountain has been restored, it no longer has its original height of 12 meters.

The group of buildings near the fountain is a bath complex, originally built in the first century CE, but restored in the fourth century by an Ephesian woman, **Scholastikia**, whose name it now carries. The dressing room (apodyterium), cold room (frigidarium), warm room (tepidarium), and hot room (caldarium) are grouped in a circular pattern, so that the frequenters of the baths would reach the entrance again after making the circuit of the various rooms. The structure had two entrances, both of which opened onto the apodyterium. The statue of the patroness, Scholastikia, decorates the

Baths of Scholastikia

main niche of this room. Including the ground floor, the building had three stories. The clay pipes that conducted hot air through the baths are still visible along the walls and on the floor of the tepidarium. West of the bath, a narrow road leads to one of the public toilets (**latrina**) in the city. One could hold long conversations in this community toilet. A basin surrounded by four columns stands in the middle of the structure. Mosaics covered the floor. A water channel ran in front of the openings that line the walls. A roof covered the area comprising the toilets themselves, while the basin stood open to the sky.

One of the most beautiful structures along Kouretes Street is the so-called **Temple of Hadrian**, which P. Quintilius built before 138 CE and dedicated to Hadrian. At a later point, statues of the emperors of the tetrarchy, Diocletian, Maximian, Constantius I, and Galerius (293-305 CE) were erected on the bases in front of the temple. The temple consists of a pronaos (porch) and a naos (main room). Two square posts stand on either corner of the façade of the pronaos, with two round columns in the middle supporting a curved arch, in the middle of which is a bust of the city goddess, Tyche.

Over the entrance to the naos itself a human figure, perhaps Medusa, is rising from a bundle of acanthus leaves. A frieze depicting important events in the history of the city decorates both sides of the pronaos interior. The original, in four parts, is on display in the museum. For many years, people assumed that this small temple in the center of the city must be the imperial neokorate ("temple warden") temple granted to the city under Hadrian. This now appears doubtful. Hadrian probably visited Ephesus three times, and it hardly seems possible that the Ephesians would have honored him with such a small temple. Between 1984-86, archaeologists uncovered a massive structure in the northwest part of the city, the Olympieion, which was probably the second neokorate temple.

Terrace houses and surround area

Terrace houses: Diagonally across the street from the Temple of Hadrian, one can see a row of shops, and behind them, private houses. These are the "terrace houses," or "the houses of the rich," since only rich people could afford such houses in the middle of the city.

The slope is laid out in terraces, on each of which two houses stand next to one another on an "island"; each island is bounded on the east and west side by streets giving access to the houses, in a sort of checkerboard pattern (the "Hippodamian plan").

The exteriors of the houses were left quite plain, while inside, the highest standards of comfort for the time held sway. Typical of Roman architectural style, the terrace houses had interior courtyards (peristyles) in the center that were open to the sky, and around which the rooms and other areas of the house grouped themselves. The light coming from the open peristyle illuminated the rooms, some of which remained dim or even quite dark because of this. The heating system was similar to that in the baths: clay pipes beneath the floors and behind the walls conducted hot air through the house. The houses also had hot and cold running water. The toilets were similar to the public ones in Ephesus, only smaller: in the houses, as well, several people could use them at the same time. The system of drainage was relatively sophisticated. Waste water flowed through pipes to the street, and from there, to the main drainage pipe beneath Kouretes Street. The terrace houses, which were constructed during the reign of Augustus, were inhabited until the seventh century CE. At that point, the houses were filled in with earth, and used as supports for water-driven mills.

Two of these houses have been excavated, restored, and made open to the public. The first is known as "House A." It stands on a plot of land measuring 900 square meters. It once had two stories, but nothing of the upper one remains.

The main entrance led to the foyer, and to the ground floor, which consisted of twelve rooms. On one side of the fountain in the foyer, a staircase led to the upper story. An arch leads from the foyer to the peristyle. Four columns surround the peristyle, which was left open to the sky. North of the peristyle are the remains of a fountain, and behind this, two rooms, the floors of which are decorated with mosaics, and the walls, with frescoes. East of the peristyle is a room with extensive frescoes, the so-called Theater Room. On the right is a scene from the "Sikyonioi" by Menander, and on the left, a scene from Euripides' "Orestes." A further fresco depicts the struggle between the river god, Akhelaos, and Herakles, over the favors of Deianeira. Mosaics cover the floor of this room. The bath and, next to it, the kitchen, lie south of this room.

One reaches "House B," with its two peristyles, from "House A." Peristyle B1 is better preserved. Its columns have Corinthian capitals made to the highest

House B

standards of ancient stonemasonry. Both black and white, as well as colored mosaics, decorate the court in front of the basin. Behind it is a particularly beautiful mosaic. It portrays Triton with his trident, the symbol of his father, Poseidon, in his left hand. With his right, he holds the reins of a seahorse, on which a Nereid (sea nymph) sits. In the center of the peristyle is a well, surrounded by a basin that collected rainwater. Southwest of the peristyle, a staircase led to the upper story. South of the peristyle is the area called the "tablinium," the most beautiful part of the house, the vaulted roof of which is covered with a mosaic. The rooms on the east have floors paved with mosaics, and frescoes on the walls. Other rooms include the "Room of the Muses," the bedroom, the kitchen, the toilet, the dining room, and the service room. In the "Room of the Muses," one sees frescoes portraying Thalia, the muse of comedy, Terpsikhore, the muse of dance, and Melpomene, the muse of tragedy. In the kitchen is the "mesura," the stone that regulated the distribution of water and drainage. If water was not needed in one room or another, the openings of the "mesura" could be closed. An arched entrance leads to the toilets, which had space for use by several people at the same time. Frescoes with male figures decorate both walls. Over their heads are the proverbial remarks, "Wait for the appropriate moment, or die," and "five before nine."

In the Roman period, hospitality held high significance. Thus, the dining room was particularly beautifully appointed. Statues of influential ancestors were prominently displayed. It was the custom that the host, after dinner, would present laudatory speeches about his family. Servants used both the dining room, called the "triclinium," and the service room to wait upon the guests.
In front of the terrace houses, directly across the street from the Temple of Hadrian, stands a monumental tomb called the **Octagon**. Archaeologists discovered the tomb in 1926. In it were

Peristyl of House B

THEATER AND SURROUNDING AREA

the skeletal remains of an 18- to 20-year-old woman. It was indeed the custom to erect statues of influential citizens in the city center, but very few were allowed to build their tombs here. This young woman must thus have been from a wealthy and important family. Recently, an interesting hypothesis has been presented: the woman could be Arsinoe IV, a princess of the Egyptian royal family. Her older sister, Cleopatra VII, was unpopular with her constituency, so Arsinoe was able to muster some support for her claim to the throne. She either fled to Ephesus, or was sent into exile by Cleopatra. She sought sanctuary in the Ephesian temple of Artemis. Like all sanctuaries, it offered immunity to fugitives seeking protection. Despite this, the princess died in Ephesus; she may even have been murdered. Since there is no tradition about a similar noble woman from this period of time, the hypothesis may well be correct. It remains unknown who built the structure. Perhaps her sister erected the tomb to whitewash the murder of Arsinoe, or perhaps Arsinoe's friends had it built; either hypothesis could explain the peculiarity of the architecture.

The octagonal monumental tomb rises from a square foundation. Eight columns with Ionian capitals surround the structure. The roof was pyramidal. The sarcophagus is in the grave chamber.

An interesting structure known as the **brothel** stands at the intersection of Kouretes Street and the marble road. The building opens onto the marble road. The first story of the two-story house is in a relatively good state of preservation. An inscription, the frescoes, and the statue of Priapos with his disproportionately large sex organ all lead to the conclusion that this was probably a brothel.

Across from the brothel, the lower columns of the monumental **Gate of Hadrian**, with its three arches, are visible; this structure was dedicated to the emperor during his lifetime. The gate leads to the terrace houses, and to

Library of Celsus

Ortygia, the place thought to be the birthplace of Artemis.

Kouretes Street ends at the **Library of Celsus**, one of the most beautiful buildings at Ephesus. This library, which dates to around 110 CE, was probably intended to be a monumental tomb for Celsus from his son, Gaius Julius Aquila. But it seems that, by this time, the construction of a tomb in the city center was allowed only if it was placed in the context of a public building, such as a library. The structure rises from a nine-stepped podium. The highly ornamented façade received special attention. Columns decorate the two-storied façade. Between the aediculae of the lower story are three entrances, the middle of which is the highest. Statues symbolizing the characteristics of Celsus stand in the niches between the columns on the lower story. These are the wisdom (Sophia), knowledge (Episteme), thought (Ennoia), and virtue (Arete) of Celsus. The statues are copies of the originals, which are now in the Ephesus Museum in Vienna.

The Turkish sultans were completely indifferent to the first excavations in Ephesus. The British architect J. T. Wood began searching for the remains of the temple of Artemis in 1869, under the aegis of the British Museum. The finds that he brought back with him to Europe awakened so great an interest that many European archaeologists immediately developed an interest for Ephesus and other ancient sites in Anatolia.

From 1874 onward, ancient finds were divided according to this system: the finder kept one-third of them, the Turkish state, one-third, and the owner of the land on which they were found, one-third. In 1895, the Austrian Otto Benndorf came to Ephesus and bought the entire plot of land on which the ruins of ancient Ephesus stood. He began excavations immediately. At the same time, the excavations in the Temple of Artemis continued under the Englishman D. G. Hogarth. The Austrians shipped all

Marble road

of their finds to Vienna, with the justification that it would be impossible to protect them from destruction in Turkey. When the Austrians began, however, to prepare a particularly priceless bronze statue found in the harbor gymnasium for shipment to Vienna, some Turkish officials raised objections. The director of the museum immediately informed the Pasha.

The dispute continued for some time, but the Turkish government and the Austrian archaeologists reached a temporary solution. From that moment, a Turkish commissar exercised oversight over the excavations. He informed the government in Istanbul that the Austrians were exporting ancient finds out of the country. Ethem Bey, the representative of the director of the Istanbul museum, came to Ephesus immediately. He was able to take a look at Otto Benndorf's finds, but did not prevent them from being sent to Vienna despite all this, because the Pasha, working for another branch of the Turkish government, gave Benndorf permission to do so. Ancient finds were thus allowed to leave the country indiscriminately because of political infighting in the government.

The founder of the Turkish museums, Osman Hamdi Bey, and his friends fought with all their effort against such measures. After the creation of a constitutional state, the Austrians no longer received permission to excavate. Turkish officials only granted the permit after the Austrians was willing to return some of their finds. These are now on display in the Archaeological Museum in Istanbul. After the foundation of the Turkish Republic, the constitution entirely forbade the export of ancient finds from the country.

Although the façade of the Library of Celsus has two stories, the inner room (10.92 by 16.72 meters) has a mere balcony instead of a second and third story. The walls behind the bookcases were hollow, perhaps to prevent moisture from damaging the scrolls. The library could contain more than 12,000 scrolls.

Commercial agora

36

The grave chamber of Celsus is beneath the ground floor, directly across from the entrance.

Immediately to the right of the Library of Celsus is a gate with three passageways, which **Mazeus and Mithridates** built. Both were slaves of the emperor Augustus, who manumitted them. In gratitude for their freedom, they built this gate. In the inscription, they dedicate the structure to the emperor, his wife Livia, his daughter Julia, and her husband Agrippa.

The gate leads to the **commercial agora**, or the "lower" agora, as the second marketplace in Ephesus is called. This square field was once the center of commerce in the city. Rows of shops, some of them two-storied, lined three sides of the plaza, in the center of which stood a sundial and a water-clock. The agora was first laid out in the third century BCE, but the ruins date from the reign of Caracalla (211-217 CE).

One of the most interesting temples, the **Temple of Serapis**, lies southwest of the agora, at the top of a flight of stairs. Serapis was an Egyptian god. Good trade relations between Ephesus and Egypt resulted in their cultural and religious influence on the Ephesians. In contrast to most Greeks and Romans, the Egyptians had a strongly developed belief in the afterlife. Perhaps for this reason, the Egyptian gods found a following among the Ephesians, and they built temples for them, one of which is the Temple of Serapis. Another hypothesis is that colonists from Egypt paid to have this temple constructed. The temple has massive walls. It consists of a naos and a pronaos.

The agora borders the so-called **marble road**, which is a portion of the sacred way that leads past Panayirdaqi to the Temple of Artemis. The marble road extends from the theater to the library. Near the theater, one can still see the tracks of Roman wagons and drainage channels on either side. The treatment of the two sides of the street is strikingly different.

Temple of Serapis

One side has a colonnade, but the level of the other was raised by two meters during the reign of Nero, upon which was built a stoa.

The **theater**, the most impressive structure in the city, lies on the west slope of Panayirdaqi. It was built during the reign of Lysimachos, and was converted into a Roman-style theater during the Roman period.

The theater served not only purposes of entertainment; people also gathered here for religious, political, and philosophical discussions. Theaters were also the scenes of gladiatorial contests and animal fights.

The theater in Ephesus is among the largest in Anatolia. It could accommodate 24,000 spectators. The cavea has sixty-six rows of seats; two diazoma divide them into three horizontal sections. The cavea is larger than semi-circular, and contains special seats for influential citizens directly in front of the orchestra. The three-storied stagehouse, eighteen meters high, was impressively decorated. Columns, between which were niches containing statues, ornamented the interior façade. Two passageways in the parodoi on either side of the stagehouse led to the seating area.

Many emperors financed the various renovations of this theater. During the reign of Claudius in the first century CE, the structure found its new Roman form. Trajan, Nero, and Domitian each contributed to its restoration and partial restructuring.

The **fountain** outside the theater to the right has Hellenistic characteristics, and dates to the second century BCE. It once had a basin with two columns, and was expanded by two additional columns in the fourth century CE.

The 530-meter harbor street runs between the theater and the harbor; this road was renamed the "Arkadiane," or "Arcadian way," after the emperor Arcadius (395 and 408 CE), the son of Theodosius I, who restored it.

Reconstruction of harbor street (Arkadiane)

Colonnades, behind which were rows of shops, lined both sides of the street, which was eleven meters wide. The waste water of the city flowed into the sea through the drainage channels beneath the street. Potable water flowed through water pipes beneath the shops.

The four marble column drums in the middle of the street were set up in the fourth century CE. The statues of the four evangelists probably once stood here.

An inscription tells us that this street was lit by night; only Ephesus, Rome and Antioch could afford to light their streets at night. For those traveling across Anatolia, the "royal highway" began with the Arkadiane, where one disembarked from ships to travel to the interior.

A monumental gate at the end of the harbor street led to the harbor itself. Because of erosion along the bed of the Kaystros river (the lesser Menderes), the harbor silted up over the course of the centuries and separated Ephesus further and further from the sea; despite all efforts to the contrary, the harbor was eventually lost. All that remains is a marshy area about 4.5 meters wide, with a small pond. Several sports facilities once lined the harbor street between the harbor and the theater.

The **theater gymnasium**, in front of the theater, is the largest in Ephesus. Colonnaded galleries lined three sides of the palaestra, which measured 30 by 70 meters. The spectators' stands occupied the fourth side. With its facilities such as its baths, classrooms, library, and lecture halls, it is an extensive complex. The imperial cult room is on the north side, the central of five rooms.

Immediately behind this gymnasium is a training field that measures 200 by 240 meters, named after **Verulanus**, chief priest of the province of Asia and the man who financed its renovation during the reign of Hadrian. The side

Sports facilities along the harbor street

of the training field nearest the harbor abuts the **harbor gymnasium**, the palaestra of which measures 20 by 40 meters. This structure had two stories and dates to the time of Hadrian. It was here that the Austrians found the priceless bronze statue of an athlete, which caused such dispute when they transported it to Vienna, as was described earlier.

The harbor bath, connected to the harbor gymnasium, is one of the largest such complexes in Ephesus. It measures 160 by 170 meters, and was 28 meters high in some places. The baths date from the second century and were restored at a later time.

Ephesus was always an important religious center, also in Christian times. The **Church of Mary**, which was built after the important councils that convened in Ephesus in 431 and 449, lies north of the harbor bath-gymnasium complex. The structure measures 260 by 20 meters, and went through four building phases. During Roman times, the building may have been a museion, a center for medical education, or it may have been the south stoa of an imperial cult temple complex dedicated to Hadrian. In this phase, the building was a three-aisled basilica. In the second phase, at the end of the fifth century, the basilica was expanded by an apse built towards its east end, its west end was converted into an atrium, and a cruciform baptisterion was added onto the north wall. In the center of the baptisterion was a baptismal font, and near this room were three additional rooms for various liturgical functions. In the time of Justinian (sixth century), a domed church was built between the apse and the narthex. In the tenth century, a small chapel was added on the south side of the church.

The ruins near the so-called "lower gate" were once a Byzantine **palace**. The hill north of this would most likely be the ancient **akropolis**. A wall surrounded it. The foundation stones of a building found near here date to the seventh to sixth centuries BCE, and thus belong to one of the oldest structures yet found at Ephesus.

The **stadium** is one of the most important buildings of the city. Sporting events took place here into the third and fourth centuries. At this time, the Romans seemed to be wild about bloodbaths. They set gladiators to compete against one another, or threw victims to confront wild beasts, which the audience eagerly watched. The animals and their human opponents were pushed through doors into the arena, where their struggle for survival began. It is possible

that the audience actually cheered on the wild beasts, since they seemed to have had little sympathy for the human competitors, who were often Christians, and thus not worshippers of Artemis. It seems that the Christians, in retaliation, destroyed the stadium, because it fell to ruin as soon as Christianity became the official religion. The stadium measures 230 meters in length and 30 meters wide, and has the form of a horseshoe. It was constructed in the Hellenistic period, and received its final form under Nero (54-68 CE).

The **Vedius Gymnasium** lies north of the stadium. This was a project funded by P. Vedius Antoninus and his wife, Flavia Papiana, members of the influential Vedius family; they dedicated the structure to Artemis and to the emperor, Antoninus Pius. One approaches the structure from its rear side today. A colonnaded portico decorated the main entrance, which was on the south side. Stoas ringed the courtyard; the stoa on the west side had two stories. The imperial cult room measured 10 by 20 meters. Various rooms, such as baths and latrines, adjoined this.

The Grotto of the Seven Sleepers:

In the year 250 CE, seven young Christians were forced to flee Ephesus. Since they were Christians of conviction, they refused to bring offerings to the imperial temples. In their fear of persecution, they hid in a cave, only to fall into a deep sleep. When they awoke, some two hundred years later, Christianity had prevailed.

The seven men continued their lives in Ephesus, and were buried in the same cave after they died.

Later, a church was erected over their tombs. Respect for these young men became so great that many worshippers desired to be buried near them. In the excavations in 1927-28, archaeologists found hundreds of graves. A path leads from the Vedius Gymnasium to the Grotto of the Seven Sleepers.

The House of Mary:

Christians have always wondered about the final resting place of the Virgin Mary. Ancient tradition has it that she died and was buried in Ephesus. The ecumenical council of 431, held in Ephesus, determined that the Virgin Mary came to Ephesus along with John the Evangelist, and lived and died there.

Visions seen by the German nun, Katherina Emmerich, confirmed this tradition; people followed her visions and found the site. This woman was a simple nun who never left her cell. In her old age, she was considered to be holy, which seldom happens during the lifetime of nuns. In 1818, she received visions of the Virgin Mary, which were sketched by C. Brentano. Katherina Emmerich made the following statement about the House of Mary: when the Christians faced increasing persecution, the Virgin Mary fled along with John from Jerusalem to Ephesus.

In 1891, Eugen Paulin, the director of the college in {zm[r and superior of the

Grotto of the Seven Sleepers

Lazarists, decided to investigate the visions of Katharina Emmerich.
He commissioned a priest, Henry Jung, to go to Ephesus with a committee of monks.

After a series of investigations, they found the House of Mary on Bülbüldağı according to the descriptions of the visionary.

News spread all over the world about the discovery, and the archbishop Timoni, in 1892, allowed commemorative services to be held in the House of Mary. Pope John XXIII declared the house to be a site of pilgrimage in 1961. Pope Paul VI made a pilgrimage to the house in 1967, as did Pope John Paul II in 1979.

Hundreds of Christians visit the house daily. The House of Mary is not only a place of pilgrimage for Christians, however; Muslims, who honor Mother Mary as the mother of Isa Peygamber, "Jesus the Prophet," undertake pilgrimages to this site as well.
In the Byzantine period, the House of Mary was converted into a cruciform basilica, of which only ruins were found.

This structure has since been restored, according to its original cruciform plan. A red line is visible on the surface of the walls; the original masonry reaches up to that point.

The statue of the Virgin Mary was installed in the apse about a hundred years ago. The room next to this apse is considered to have been her bedroom. There was once a further room, symmetrically placed on the other side of the apse.

A garden surrounds the house; about a hundred meters from the house is a cistern with ruins of walls.

In the garden are several wells, the water of which is reputed to have healing power.

House of the Virgin Mary

Museum: The Ephesus Museum in Selçuk is devoted entirely to finds from Ephesus and the immediately surrounding area, which date to the Mycenean, archaic, classical, Hellenistic, Roman, Byzantine, and Turkish eras.

Hall of house finds: In the course of excavations at the so-called Temple of Hadrian, archaeologists discovered the terrace houses, which date to the Roman period, when Ephesus was one of the key cities of the empire. Objects found in the houses, which were inhabited from the first to seventh centuries CE, are on display in this room.

The showcases on the left chiefly contain small household objects, portrait busts, and statuettes of gods and emperors. Along the left wall are the statues of the gods Bes, Priapos, and Eros, along with portrait busts of the famous playwright Menander, and a head of Sokrates. Directly across from the entrance of the room are a statue of Artemis the huntress, and some of the wall frescoes from the terrace houses.

Along the right wall, one finds the head of a priestess, followed by a bronze bust

displaying especially fine workmanship; this may be a portrait of a philosopher. In the center of the room are the three most important works of art in the museum. One of these is a

Eros,
the bust of
Sokrates,
Eros riding
a dolphin

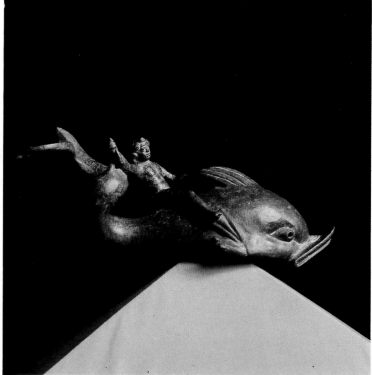

second-century CE statue of Eros riding a dolphin. These sorts of figures were commonly used for the spouts of fountains. The second work is a statue of an Egyptian priest, dating to the sixth century BCE. The third work of art is a Roman copy of the head of Eros made by the famous ancient sculptor Lysippos.

Hall of fountain finds: This room displays finds from the fountains of Pollio, Trajan, and Gaius Laecanius Bassus. Directly left of the entrance is a bust of Zeus and a statue of Aphrodite. In the center of the room is the statue of the resting warrior. To the far left, one can see the statue group of Odysseus and Polyphemos, which was found at the Fountain of Pollio. When Odysseus and his companions were journeying homeward after the end of the Trojan war, a storm blew them off course and onto the island of the man-eating giant, Polyphemos. Odysseus' friends managed to get the monster drunk. They were then able to poke out his one eye and flee. The giant Polyphemos stands in the center of the group, with Odysseus next to him on the left. On either side of

statue of an Egyptian priest, and the god Bes

them, Odysseus' companions are busily bringing more wine and sharpening a wooden post.

The statues displayed across from this group once stood in the Fountain of

45

Trajan. The first shows Dionysos leaning on a tree stump. Other statues from this fountain are the reclining satyr, Aphrodite holding a seashell against her navel, and Androklos with his dog. Along the wall on the right is a series of portrait busts, across from which are statues from the Fountain of Gaius Laecanius Bassus.

Hall of recent finds: Recently-found objects are usually displayed here for a few years. Immediately right of the entrance is a showcase containing finds that date primarily to the Byzantine Christian period. Further right is a fine collection of coins and valuable jewelry. Until the Roman period, Ephesian coins displayed a bee, the symbol of the city, on one side, and Artemis in cultic garb on the other side. In the Roman period, the head of the emperor or one of his relatives appeared on one side, and buildings or other symbols of Ephesus on the other. The masks hanging on the wall to the left of the entrance were found in the theater. Since masks were usually made of leather or wood, these stone masks were probably decorations. On the same wall is an illustration of the production of oil lamps

in Ephesus. Among the other recent finds are the figure of Eros with a mask, amphorae, statuettes of Eros, a statue of

Aphrodite and Dionysos

46

Aphrodite, and various portrait busts. The rarest object in this room is a three-paneled ivory frieze from the terrace houses, which portrays Trajan's war against the barbarians in the East, and preparations for it.

Garden: This is a lovely area well suited to the surroundings of the museum. On the right are sarcophagi, funerary reliefs, altars, and inscriptions. Among them is an interesting decorated sarcophagus from the second or third century CE. Figures of the muses ornament the sides. According to the inscription, the sarcophagus was used a second time in the Byzantine period. Funerary reliefs and votive steles also line the west side of the garden. The votive steles express the good wishes of the person making the commemoration, whereas the funerary reliefs portray the relatives of the deceased saying their final farewell.

In the center of the garden is a semicircular sundial with an engraved scale for the hours. The scale is divided into twelve evenly-spaced sections. The shadow of the pointer indicates the time.

The clock would have been turned to accommodate the position of the sun as it changed over the seasons of the year.

Dionysos, the reclining varrior

47

Hall of grave finds: This room, which opens onto the garden, displays graves and grave gifts. On the right wall is an illustration of the various burial practices customary in Anatolia. Finds from a Mycenean grave discovered in front of the St. John complex are on display in the first showcase on the left. These hold great significance for the history of Ephesus, because they demonstrate that a settlement existed here long before Androklos founded the city, for the small grave gifts date from the fourteenth to twelfth centuries BCE. Glass objects from graves in Ephesus and the surrounding area are in the other showcases. A number of sarcophagi and ossuaries are on display in this room. On the walls are reliefs illustrating funerary customs. The grave relief of Olympia, the daughter of Diokles, which dates from the second century BCE, is of particular interest. The façade of a building in the Doric style frames the stele, and surrounds the relief of a woman, who is holding her head covering shut with her right hand.

The hall of Artemis: Statues of Artemis and cultic objects relating to the goddess are on display in this room. Two particularly beautiful statues reflect her glory. These were found, by complete chance, buried in the prytaneion, and date to the first and second centuries CE. The statue on the left is known as the "large Artemis." She wears a headdress (polos) with three zones, one of which contains Ionic-order temples, and the others, sphinxes and griffins. Beneath two rows of necklaces are three rows of round protuberances, which are symbols of fertility; according to the latest hypothesis, these could be the testicles of sacrificial bulls. Her lower arms are missing. Around her waist is a belt with bee motifs. Rectangular fields, which contain portrayals of various types of animals, cover her skirt.

The "beautiful Artemis" stands across the room from the "large Artemis." True to her name, she was fashioned of better marble and shows a higher quality of

Stele, the consul Stephanos

workmanship. The sacred deer and honeycombs stand on either side of her. Her skirt reaches to her feet; as with the other statue, animal motifs predominate. The protuberances begin immediately above her waist. The symbols of the zodiac are carved beneath her necklace, and figures of Nike (goddess of victory) stand above it. This statue has no headdress. Next to this statue is the "little Artemis," a statue that dates to about the same period. Finds from the Temple of Artemis fill the showcases. Among them is a statuette of a ram from the period of the Kimmerians. The large stone horse belongs to a team that stood near the altar of the temple; this dates to the fourth century BCE.

Hall of imperial cult finds: Portrait busts and statues of emperors and their relatives comprise the chief contents of this room. A few of these, surprisingly, have crosses scratched onto their foreheads. Christians inscribed them after the official recognition of their religion, perhaps as a form of exorcism performed on the statues. To the right of the entrance is the statue of Stephanos, a consul, who is on the point of dropping a handkerchief to signal the beginning of a race. On the left wall is an illustration of the so-called Temple of Hadrian; on both sides of it are the original friezes of the temple. The various friezes portray Androklos and his hunt for the wild boar, the Amazons, a Dionysiac scene, and a portrait of various gods and heroes, among them Athena, the moon goddess Selene, Apollo, Androklos, Herakles, and Artemis.

A portion from the altar of the Temple of Domitian is also on display. This altar was U-shaped and had friezes on three sides. On the front face are Asiatic armor and weapons, and on the sides, a sacrificial bull stands before the altar, and further shields and weapons appear. Near the exit of the room are fragments of a monumental statue of the emperor Domitian, as well as statues of Augustus and his wife, Livia, and portions of the Parthian monument.

Parts of the monumental statue of Domitian

THE ISA BEY MOSQUE

This mosque is a lovely example of the transition between Seljuk and Ottoman architecture. It rises imposingly among the Roman and Byzantine (Eastern Roman) monuments, as though in conscious attempt to allow this building to compete with them.

The Syrian architect Ali built the mosque in 1375, on a commission from Isa Bey, a member of the ruling family Aydinoqlu. In its construction, the usual rules of symmetry were ignored.

This characteristic guides a seeming neglect of all that was customary in mosque architecture before it: the gate is not in the center of the structure, and the doors, windows, and domes do not match one another. Despite this, the Isa Bey mosque has the same significance for the architecture of Selçuk that the Mosque of Süleyman carries for Istanbul, and the Mosque of Selim for Edirne.

The mosque consists of an inner courtyard and a house of prayer. Colonnades surround three sides of the courtyard, with a prominent wadirvan in its center, for ceremonial washing. The main entrance is on the west side.

The most interesting ornamental feature of the mosque, the mihrab, is now in a mosque in Izmir, because the Isa Bey Mosque fell out of use for some time. After this rather strange occurrence, the people of Selçuk had no choice but to build a new mihrab. According to Evliya Çelebi, the minbar was once lined with walnut.

The columns and their capitals are like a tour of antiquity; most of them come from earlier ruins in Ephesus. Turquoise and blue faience decorate the domes, which are primarily white.

The Fortress:
This stands out prominently like the crown of the entire city. Embodying the pride and honor of its 1500-year history, it silently emanates security and peace even today.

As mentioned above, the Ephesians, at the close of antiquity, withdrew to the hill of Ayasuluk and erected this fortress. This is thus a Byzantine (Eastern Roman Imperial) structure.

During the emirate of the Aydinoqlu family and the Ottoman empire, this was still a significant fortress, and was rebuilt and altered many times.

Isa Bey Mosque

The Church of St. John:

According to tradition, John became the leader of the church in Ephesus after Paul's death, and he wrote his gospel and died there. According to tradition, during his lifetime, he expressed the wish to be buried on Ayasuluk hill. Three hundred years after his death, a small basilica was built over his tomb. In the sixth-century heyday of the Byzantine empire, the emperor Justinian, who wished to honor John the Evangelist in a more appropriate way, built a very imposing basilica over the site of the small church.

The power of the Byzantine empire weakened, however, from time to time, resulting in the occupation of its lands by hostile powers. Ephesus was also subject to this. Arabs occupied the city in the seventh and eighth centuries. The Ephesians tried to defend both themselves and their church, and thus constructed a fortress around the church and its grounds. The Ottomans later came to Anatolia and spread Islam. As a result, the Church of St. John lost its significance. This state of affairs, of course, did not please the Christians. The income from pilgrimages to the site also declined. Testimonies that the dust emanating from the evangelist's grave chamber had miraculous healing power, however, did continue to bring pilgrims. Christians in search of healing came in droves from the surrounding areas. Muslims also later came to the site for the same reason. The church was used as a mosque for a short time in the fourteenth century, though it fell victim to an earthquake later in the same century.

After the First World War, Greek forces occupied the greater part of the Aegean coast. During this period of upheaval, the Greek archaeologist Soteriou began excavations at the Church of St. John on Ayasuluk. Excavations are still continuing here, and a great part of the structure has been restored already.

A wall with twenty towers and three gates protected the church. The most important entrance is the so-called Gate of Persecution, through which one enters the complex today. A further gate is on the east, and another on the west.

The Gate of Persecution, which has two doors, opens onto a small courtyard that also served defensive purposes. This connects with the atrium, which measures 34 by 47 meters, from which one can enter the three-aisled basilica. Three small domes once covered the narthex. It leads to the nave (main aisle) of the

church; colonnades separate it from the side aisles. On the front face of some of the columns, one can see the monogram of the emperor Justinian and his wife, Theodora, a clear sign that the emperor financed this church. Arches connected the columns on the lower story, on top of which the columns of the second story stood. The church has a cruciform plan. Six domes once covered the main part of the church. At the end of the nave is an apse, in front of which is the tomb of Saint John, beneath a two-stepped podium. The four columns at its corners once carried a dome.

North of the church is a room, the upper part of which is temporarily closed. This was the treasury, or sacristy, part of which was converted into a chapel in the tenth century. The apse of the chapel carries frescoes. By means of a door in the chapel, one enters the remaining part of the sacristy. In front of this structure is a complex of three rooms, which was the baptisterion. The round baptismal font is built into the floor of the octagonal room.

PLAN
OF
EPHESUS

1. Vedius Gymnasium
2. Stadium
3. Church of the Blessed Virgin
4. Port Gymnasium
5. Baths
6. Arcadian Way
   (Harbour Street)
7. Verulanus Sports Ground
8. Theatre-Gymnasium
9. Theatre
10. Marble Way
11. Celsus Library
12. Mazaeus and
    Mithridates Gate
13. Commercial Agora
14. Serapis Temple
15. Hill Houses
16. Brothel
17. Latrine
18. Hadrian Temple

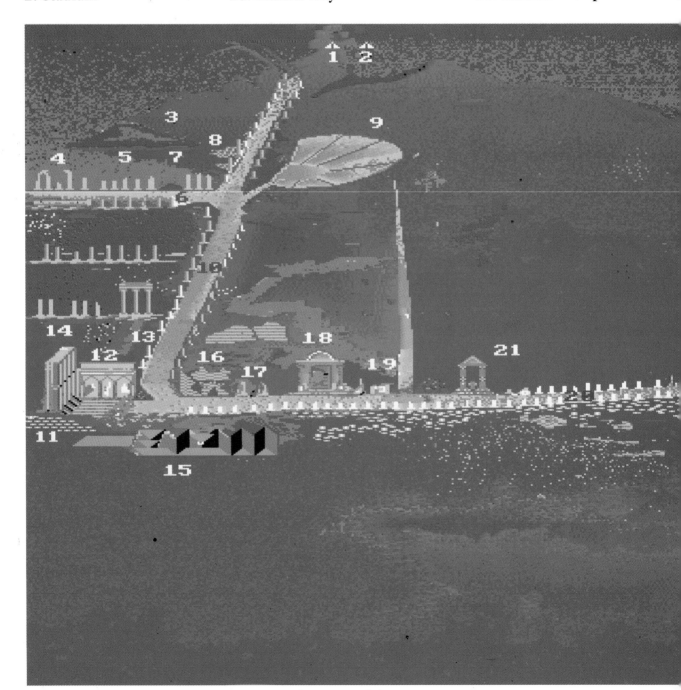

DOĞAN GÜMÜŞ
Philologist and Art History

Translation
Christine M. Thomas

Photographs
Doğan Gümüş, Şemsi Güner, Enis Üçbaylar, Serdar Çelenk, Aşkın Sağıroğlu

---

Designer
Ertan İrgin

Recondition
Semra Hasgüleç, Hüdai Özgüder

Coloured Reproduction
Çali Grafik

Printed in Istanbul by
SEÇİL OFSET

Published **DO-GÜ** Yayıncılık Turizm Ticaret Ltd. Şti.
Göktaş Sok. Göktaş Apt. 8/2 Çemberlitaş-İstanbul
Tel: (0-212) 516 59 47 - 516 20 74, Fax: (0-212) 516 59 47

1996